OUR AGRICULTURAL HERITAGE

A SELECTION OF FARM MACHINERY RESTORED

Illustrations **Peter Hawke**

Text **Emma Wood**

Sponsored by **Esso Petroleum Company Limited**

2

Editorial Consultants
Michael Oliver, Jonathan Minns

Photography
Norman Tinkler, p19, Barry Finch, p27, p30

Designed by
Barry Jones

© Esso Petroleum Company Ltd./Queen Anne Press Ltd.
First published by the Queen Anne Press Ltd. in 1971

Published by the Queen Anne Press,
Paulton House, 8 Shepherdess Walk, London N1
Printed and bound in Great Britain by
Chromoworks Ltd, Wigman Road, Aspley, Nottingham

SBN 362 00097 2   £1.75

CONTENTS

ACKNOWLEDGEMENTS

4

The author is indebted to numerous individuals
and organisations without whose
co-operation and advice this book could not
have been written, and in particular:

Miss Sadie Ward, Assistant Keeper, Reading
    Museum of Rural Life
Mrs Lesley West, Assistant Keeper, Science
    Museum, South Kensington
The Hampshire County Museum Service
R. Corbett, The Tasker Trust
M. E. Williams, Ransomes, Sims and Jefferies Ltd.
J. Hutchinson. Marshall-Fowler Ltd.
W. F. Overman, International Harvester Company
Richard Peskett, Treasurer, Worthing and
    Southern Counties Historic Vehicle Group
Ran Hawthorn, Editor, *Steaming*
The staff of *Esso Farmer*
Mrs. J. W. Harris, Paragon Petroleum Ltd.,
    Brentwood, Essex
B. C. Fitch and R. Alderton, Spencer Abbot
    (Petroleum) Ltd., Birmingham and Tamworth
T. A. Rutherford, Northern Farmers' Oil,
    Hexham, Northumberland
The Royal Agricultural Society
The Estate of the late C. Henry Warren for
    permission to reprint from *The Land is Yours*

FOREWORD

It seems to me most fitting that the name of Esso, so long and inextricably linked with the world of machines, should now be associated with this publication. The preservation and restoration of old farm equipment is a subject which arouses interest among young and old alike – people from all walks of life whose enthusiasm and energy make a most valuable contribution to recording the history of an important part of our agricultural heritage.

In compiling this book, the editors received offers of assistance from people throughout the country, too numerous to list. Often themselves involved in restoration, they included large numbers of farmers as well as many of our own Authorised Distributor Companies' representatives, who told of the whereabouts and histories of a wide variety of machines. I thank these contributors most warmly, and only regret that space limitations precluded our accommodating within these pages more than a small part of the information they supplied.

With such a wealth of material available, selection becomes very difficult, but I believe that the contents of this, our first book on the subject, represents a true cross-section of the most interesting machines in preservation today, as well as giving an insight into the motivation of some of the people engaged in this absorbing pastime.

Chairman, Esso Petroleum Company Limited.

PREFACE

6

Modern farming has come a long way from the days when smallholders scratched a living from the soil, literally with their own hands. Many small mixed farms still exist, but these are now almost completely mechanised. And several of today's farmers control vast acres of artificially fertilized, pest-free land at the mere touch of a button.

Yet this age of ultra-mechanisation is no sudden upheaval. It evolved slowly, over hundreds of years, until a sudden leap forward in the nineteenth century, when man learned how to harness all the available power for the good of the land.

It would be impossible in a book of this size to attempt a definitive history of early farm machinery. We have chosen therefore, to give some indication of how man's use of motive power developed throughout the ages, illustrated by examples of the machines which provided this power.

Above all, *Our Agricultural Heritage* is not simply a historical survey. Each of the machines included in this book is still very much alive, lovingly preserved by men from all parts of the country, and from all walks of life, who respect the magnificent achievements of our early agricultural pioneers. By telling the stories of how these old engines and implements progressed throughout their working life to their present owners, and the type of restoration carried out, we are paying our own small tribute to the men responsible for the present boom in preserving early farm machinery.

INTRODUCTION

In the beginning of course man had only himself and his mate to rely on. Some primitive instinct told him to stir the ground before putting in seed which he did with a simple dibbling stick. This gradually developed into a spade-like levered implement, then added handles to steer and a beam to guide. The stick had become recognisable as an early plough.

At first man pulled the plough himself, though very soon he gave way to oxen. As ploughs became lighter and more efficient they became horse-drawn, and horses began to play an indispensible role in English rural life. When not ploughing they were most often found between the shafts of a craftsman-made cart or wagon, bringing in the harvest or spreading manure.

Horses were also used for driving stationary machinery. Horse-powers were either simple geared wooden wheels whereby one animal transmitted power to several machines through a linking device, or treadmill-type belts involving two or more horses.

Horse-powers were mainly used to drive small items of barn machinery which would otherwise be worked by hand. Such machines were usually corn crushers and grinders, root slicers and pulpers and other devices for making cattle feed more easily digestible. Various kinds of dairy implements like butter churns could also be powered by horse-driven machines.

Farming continued in this gentle way well into the eighteenth century. There were earlier innovations: Jethro Tull's seed drill was to be the prototype for all modern sowing techniques, and Patrick Bell's reaper achieved the near impossible by replacing the sickle with a machine to cut corn. Yet these were isolated achievements, and it was not till iron came into general use for ploughshares, etc., that English agriculture really made the great leap forward.

The nineteenth century saw the great steam boom in the fields as well as on the roads and railways. Stationary engines, fixed to barn floors became popular for driving milking machines, etc., but their power was limited and lack of mobility was a serious drawback.

In 1841 Ransomes of Ipswich produced the first self-moving engine which, the next year, was converted into a portable threshing machine. Literally an engine on wheels it was steered by two or three horses. This was indeed the forerunner of the chain-driven steam traction engine.

For the next 20 years there was little development, but steam had come to stay. By the end of the century most of the major engineering companies were producing traction engines for agricultural use, and John Fowler's method of ploughing with two engines and a winch drum was firmly established.

Were it not for the unusual situation created by the First World War, when every possible acre of ground had to be sown, and speed was of the essence, steam power in agriculture would have had a much longer life span. But the introduction of the internal combustion engined tractor with its manoeuvrability changed all the old ways. American, and soon British-made tractors had, by the end of the war, more or less replaced steam engines for agricultural use.

The birth of the big combine harvesters changed the face of English agriculture still more, until it developed into the super-efficient, almost impersonal industry it is today. It is in an effort to combat this loss of character, that the people featured in this book are spending time and money to restore examples of those old machines which were once an integral part of English farm life. That their labours are not in vain is proved by the huge attendances at steam rallies and local fairs throughout the country. We sincerely hope that this book too will play a part, however small, in preserving our country's very fine agricultural heritage.

FOSTER PORTABLE ENGINE, NO. 201, 1870, "GREAT TEW"

GENERAL SPECIFICATION

MAKER	William Foster & Co. Ltd.
DATE	1870
PLACE OF ORIGIN	Lincoln
MACHINE TYPE	Portable
N.H.P.	8
CYLINDER TYPE	Single-cylinder
CYLINDER DIMENSIONS	10″ bore, 12″ stroke
LENGTH OVERALL	10′ 10$\frac{3}{4}$″
WIDTH OVERALL	5′ 5″
WHEELBASE	6′ 2″
FUEL	Wood
WORKING PRESSURE	80 lbs per square in.
BELT HORSEPOWER	70
DRIVE ARRANGEMENT	Watt's Centrifugal Belt
VALVE GEAR	Slide Valve

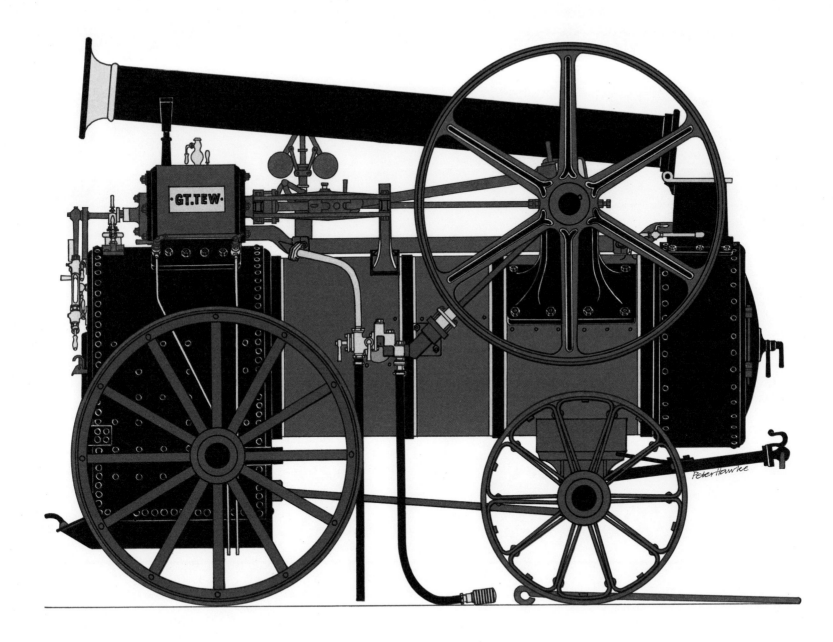

Farmers, by nature, are a conservative breed. Methods of tending the land, evolved over generations, do not give way easily to revolutionary new ideas or inventions. So it was that the first high-pressure steam engines for agricultural use were received with scant attention when developed in the early 1800s.

Richard Trevithick, "the father of the steam locomotive", most famed for his work on the mines and railways, began with an interest in road locomotion. By 1812, after succeeding with several road and stationary steam engines, he produced a portable engine for use on farms. Mounted on four wheels it weighed 15 cwt., was pulled by as many as four horses, and in fact contained all the basic principles employed in the first traction engine some 30 years later.

Selling at around 60 guineas, Trevithick's engine was thought too expensive and new-fangled by the sceptical farmers who preferred to stick to the horse-powered machines which they knew. And for many years threshing machines, corn grinders and chaff cutters continued to be motivated by various types of machinery which were mostly horse-driven (see page 13).

Indeed, when the first steam engines were produced their capacity was measured in nominal horse power (nhp) in an attempt to make matters clear to the non-mechanically minded. So a 5 nhp engine, does not simply mean that it had as much power as five horses, but that it achieved the same amount of power as one of the old machines driven by this number of horses.

Steam development continued for the next 30 years, so that by the 1860s the advantages of steam portables – the only independent form of power available – began to outweigh the initial prejudice and high cost. Comparisons between horses and steam still took place, but more and more the impressive-looking portables with their tall chimneys, huge cylindrical boilers and mighty flywheels became a common sight throughout the English countryside.

Many of the famous names of nineteenth century engineering including Clayton and Shuttleworth, Ruston and Hornsby, Ransomes, Sims and Jefferies, and Marshalls, all rode up on the steam boom. They continued to manufacture portables until the 1930s, although by the turn of the century most production was centred on the increasingly popular traction engines.

One such company was that of William Foster of Lincoln whose Wellington Foundry was renowned for precision engineering. In 1870 Fosters produced an 8 nhp portable which was sold to one John Ellis. Little more is known of Mr Ellis as only his name exists on the original record of sale. Perhaps he was a small farmer who could not really afford to run such a demanding engine – in the main portables were only used on large estates or by agricultural contractors – but, whatever the reason he only kept the Foster for a year.

The engine then passed into the hands of large land-owners at Great Tew, Oxfordshire who used it to drive a rack bench in the estate timber yard. It replaced a massive old beam engine made by Bolton and Watt, the same James Watt who invented the separate condenser as used on low-pressure steam engines, and was, in fact, an ancestor of the present Major Robb at Great Tew.

For the next 95 years the portable remained on that estate and was still working up to 1946. It then lay derelict and almost forgotten until a happy chance brought it to the attention of its present owner, Tom Gascoigne of Bodicote, near Banbury, Oxon. Tom, a garage proprietor, had been interested in steam engines for some years, and was anxious to purchase one, when he heard that the Foster was for sale for renovation although not for scrap. An arrangement was made with the then owner, Major Robb, and Tom set about the difficult task of bringing the old engine back to life in full working order.

Virtually marooned in a stone barn with a six-foot mound of earth in front of the doors, the Foster eventually saw daylight one day in 1965 after being pulled out by a tractor. 'Great Tew' as the engine is now named, was in a sorry state, as shown by photographs taken at the time and now in the Woodstock Museum. The chimney had completely deteriorated, the boiler needed retubing and the original wheels had long since been replaced by stronger ones.

However, the fact that the engine had been working indoors ensured that it was still mechanically sound, so that after a year's labour it was turned out virtually as good as new. Together with his friend, John Batsford, Tom Gascoigne worked on the Foster for a few hours every day in his spare time. A new chimney was constructed and the boiler retubed. After the rust had been rubbed down the engine was repainted in its original colours; a green body with black and yellow lines and red wheels.

When working the Foster would use as much as 250 gallons of water and 6 cwt. of coal a day, (in this case off-cuts of wood) both usually provided by the farmer. Charges for threshing, etc., obviously grew more expensive with the passing of the years, but it was impossible for some contractors to charge more than others as the National Traction Engine Users Club laid down a set scale of prices.

'Great Tew' now goes out two or three times a year to local rallies. Provided with two full-size flywheels for extra power take-off – it is not known when the second wheel was added as the original technical drawings only show one – the engine is still capable of driving a threshing drum or any machinery.

A true steam enthusiast, Tom Gascoigne is also the owner of a decorative Showman's Engine, No. 3894, 'Saint Brannock' built by the prolific company of Charles Burrell & Sons (see page 18) in 1921. Ever on the look-out for something new he recently purchased a steeple engine, well over a hundred years old, used to provide power in a local brewery. Made by Lampitts of Banbury the engine only stopped working when the brewery closed in 1950. This unusual stationary engine is often powered by steam from the portable when attending rallies.

Yet it is always the Foster – 100 years old and still going strong, is its owner's proud boast – which attracts most attention. Not surprisingly, as portable engines which run on wood like 'Great Tew' have been called the most efficient human invention ever produced, in that they can saw more wood than they burn!

'Great Tew' ready for action, with
Tom Gascoigne in the foreground

BARN MACHINERY: HORSE GEAR, 1840; OIL CAKE BREAKER, 1895; CORN GRINDER, 1920; ROOT PULPER, 1920

GENERAL SPECIFICATION

	HORSE GEAR	OIL CAKE BREAKER	ROOT PULPER	CORN GRINDER
MAKER	Perkins	Corbett & Peele	Wreckin	Bentall
DATE	1840 (approx.)	1895	1920	1920
PLACE OF ORIGIN	Hitchin, Herts.	Shrewsbury	—	Heybridge
LENGTH	64″	26″	29″	33″
WIDTH	58″	32″	29″	34″
HEIGHT	23″	52″	44″	55″
POLE	9′ 3″	—	—	—
WEIGHT	5–6 cwt.	$2\frac{1}{2}$–3 cwt.	1–$1\frac{1}{2}$ cwt.	$2\frac{1}{2}$–3 cwt.

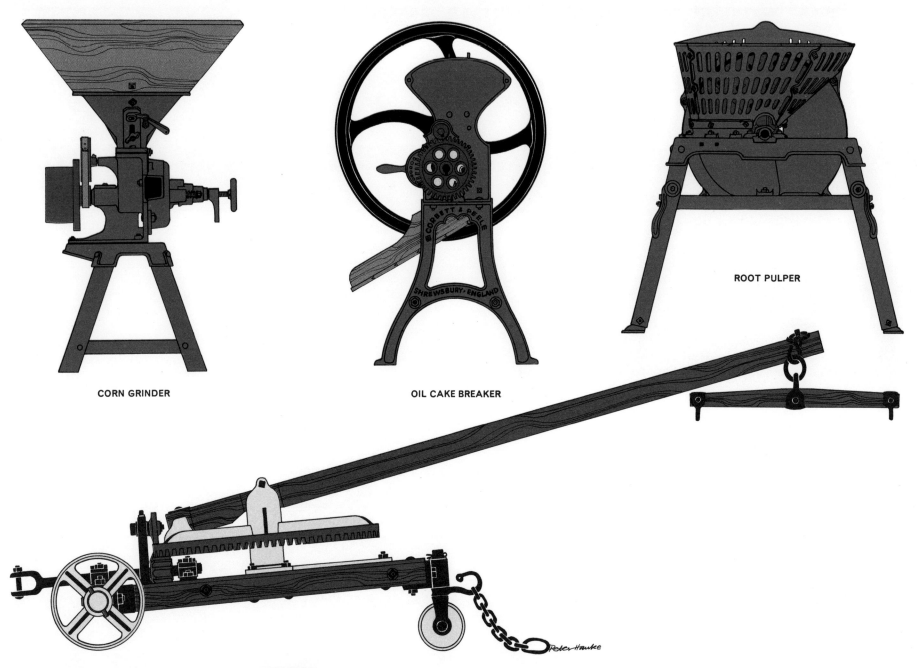

CORN GRINDER

OIL CAKE BREAKER

ROOT PULPER

HORSE GEAR

BARN MACHINERY: HORSE GEAR, 1840; OIL CAKE BREAKER, 1895; CORN GRINDER, 1920; ROOT PULPER, 1920

At a first glance Henry Jackson's garden at Tilford, near Farnham, Surrey, looks like a permanent exhibition of modern art, with weird and wonderful iron shapes in strong primary colours reposing on extensive lawns. Closer inspection reveals it to be one of the most varied and lovingly restored collections of old farm machinery in the South of England.

Starting with a Howard plough – introduced initially in the 1840s at a cost of £4 5s. – which they found in local woods and cleaned up purely for decorative purposes, Henry and his wife Madge have built up their collection in just three years to its present strength. Now they have some 45 different items of machinery, ranging from a late 1800s three-row steering hoe to a 1930 potato planter which contains technical details still being employed in the latest German model.

In a few years' time when more implements are restored Henry Jackson intends to erect a home for the machines which will serve as a local museum of rural life. This will be a museum with a difference – wherever possible the machinery will be seen working.

Although most of the glamour in farming is associated with the major crops such as wheat for milling and brewing, just as important on a day-to-day basis are the more homely products used for cattle feed. Oats, barley, beans, turnips and other crops all have to be processed to an edible consistency, a process which in the nineteenth century was carried out by both the hand-operated and horse-driven machines.

Henry Jackson owns one of the simplest and most effective forms of horse power ever used, a simple, toothed iron wheel with a wooden shaft attached, to which a horse was harnessed. By walking round in a circle the horse conveyed power through a gearing mechanism to drive between one and four small machines.

More advanced types of horse-powers involved some two or three horses working a kind of treadmill, and it was from these machines that the term nominal horse power (nhp) was culled to explain the capacity of the first steam engines (see page 10).

Mr Jackson purchased the horse gear last year from a local farmer whose family had bought it new in the early 1840s. Rusty, and without its pole, the machine has now been fitted with a new shaft and painted red and yellow. Similar one-horse powers were still in use up to the 1890s even when steam had taken over most of their functions.

One machine which could have been driven by the horse-gear and is, in the Jackson collection, placed in close proximity, is a corn grinder (pictured in our illustration on the left). Crops had to be crushed and ground to make them easily digestible by cattle. Lighter feeds such as oats were simply rolled through a machine consisting of a set of heavy rollers. Some grain was kibbled – crushed into small pieces – but sturdier crops were finely ground by a machine in which a rotating plate revolved next to a fixed one.

A machine which performed a similar function was the root pulper, shown here on the right. At first such food as turnips was fed whole to animals, but by the beginning of the nine-teenth century slicing into large pieces had become quite common. A further step of cutting into even smaller pieces made root crops more palatable to young animals who had lost their teeth. Finally the root pulper reduced the crop to a much finer matter.

These small, sturdy, effective pieces of farm equipment are known as barn machinery, as this was usually where they were found. Many of them were hand-operated like the oil cake breaker in the centre of our drawing. This particular machine, bought for £1 a year ago, was made by Corbett and Peele of Shrewsbury in 1895.

Oil cakes as cattle food were introduced at the

end of the eighteenth century. The cakes were sent to the farms in inch-thick oblong blocks, too hard to be eaten whole. So machines with toothed rollers were devised to break up the cakes, rendering them easier on the animals' teeth.

Other items in the Jackson collection include a 70-year-old threshing drum and wooden elevator, an ancient hay wain, a 1926 Massey-Harris seed drill and a hay tedder. There is also a 1900 binder, a chaff cutter, fertilizer spreader, potato bulker, hay rake, winnowing machine, dung cart and a blacksmith's forge waiting to be rebuilt.

All these pieces come from far and near. Most of the Jackson's friends and colleagues are on the look out for any examples which might enhance the collection, and when Mr and Mrs Jackson are on holiday they spend a lot of their time searching the hedgerows. Any 'find' is usually purchased at scrap value.

Whilst Henry Jackson looks after the purely mechanical side, Madge does all the painting, carefully matching colours with original shades found when rubbing down rust or going back to the makers' records to seek out the correct lining. She has just finished restoring a 1919 Wiltshire wagon, first made by local craftsmen for E. Perrett of Heytesbury.

Mrs Jackson's home reflects her interest. Inside the 300-year old cottage hang gleaming horse brasses and a horse collar. Alongside a washing machine in the modern kitchen stands an old butter churn with its highly-polished wooden barrel.

It is interesting to see a twentieth century

housewife preserving links with her counterparts a half-a-century ago. It is vital that people like Mr and Mrs Jackson are keeping us in touch with the work of the village blacksmith, a now near extinct representative of all that was best in English agricultural life until so few years ago.

BURRELL GENERAL PURPOSE TRACTION ENGINE, NO. 4048, 1926, "WILLIAM II"

GENERAL SPECIFICATION

MAKER	Charles Burrell & Sons
DATE	1926
PLACE OF ORIGIN	Thetford, Norfolk
MACHINE TYPE	General Purpose Agricultural Traction Engine
N.H.P.	7
B.H.P.	38
CYLINDER TYPE	Single-cylinder
CYLINDER DIMENSIONS	8½" bore, 12" stroke
LENGTH OVERALL	18'
WIDTH OVERALL	7' 8"
WEIGHT	12 tons 5 cwt.
WORKING PRESSURE	185 lbs per square in.
WATER TANK CAPACITY	126 gallons
FUEL	Coal, wood, straw
FUEL CAPACITY	5 cwt.
GOVERNOR TYPE	Pickering
DRIVE ARRANGEMENT	Two-speed, three shaft
BRAKE TYPE	Block
BELT HORSEPOWER	38
VALVE GEAR	Stephenson's link motion
AVERAGE SPEED	10 mph

BURRELL GENERAL PURPOSE TRACTION ENGINE, NO. 4048, 1926, "WILLIAM II"

Ask any steam enthusiast what a traction engine looks like, and he will most probably describe a General Purpose Agricultural Engine. For not only is this type of engine a most popular draw today at steam rallies throughout the country, it is also the one most remembered by old men who worked the land and younger men who, as boys, watched the big engines steaming from farm to farm along local roads.

Indeed, there were probably more General Purpose-type Traction Engines used throughout agriculture than any other type of steam engine: their sturdiness and simplicity of design enabling them to cope with a variety of different tasks. In the main these engines were used to provide governed power for threshing drums, but during the spring and summer they also drove saw benches and hauled wood from forests.

Owning a traction engine was considered uneconomical unless a farm was over 750 acres, so most engines were the property of general agricultural contractors who travelled around to farms within their local area charging set rates for threshing and haulage work. The contractors frequently provided their own threshing drum and labour also.

General Purpose Traction Engines were fitted with governors mounted on the cylinder block or weighshaft bracket and driven by belt from the crankshaft. These made the engine self-regulating when driving such machinery as a threshing drum from a stationary position by means of a belt running from the flywheel.

The other main characteristic of this kind of engine was its winch drum fixed on the rear axle, containing a wire rope of about 100 yards long. A ten-ton engine could pull 20 tons direct and winch 50 tons. The object to be moved would be winched in, the length of the rope, whilst the engine remained stationary. Then the engine would be moved forward and the rope played out again, the whole process being repeated until the object reached its destination.

Ask anyone who worked these engines to name his favourite make, and the answer, more often than not, will be that produced by the Thetford, Norfolk-based engineering firm of Charles Burrell & Sons. Founded in 1857 Burrells manufactured over 5,000 engines before going into liquidation in 1929, and there are probably more of their engines in preservation than any other make. They also built many of the highly-decorated, canopied engines used by fairground Showmen for hauling equipment and living vans on the road and powering roundabouts, etc., on site.

Men who drove Burrells in their heyday testify that they were both easy to handle and economical to run. Men who preserve them today are enamoured of their purity of line and the inherent engineering expertise.

This is certainly the case with engine no. 4048, pictured overleaf, described by one expert as "one of the finest types ever produced in this country in terms of engineering excellence". Built in 1926 it brought to perfection those basic design principles employed when the first traction engines were turned out in the 1850s.

Purchased new by a Norfolk farmer who used it for both threshing and timber work, the Burrell was later sold to one William Hillary, a contractor of Micheldever, Hants. who worked the engine solidly till 1946. During this time he fitted a copper (instead of cast-iron) chimney cap, and named the engine 'William II' after his son. It then lay derelict for nearly 20 years until purchased by its present owner, Michael Lugg of Billingshurst, Sussex from a sale in Hampshire for around £300.

Michael, a young engineer, had coveted this particular engine for many years, following its progress from one 'graveyard' to another. The fourth generation of a family of steam engineers, he owned his first traction engine at the age of 11, so his interest in the Burrell was hardly surprising. His grandfather, Oppy Lugg, who built up the family contracting business, made the name of Lugg renowned in steam circles from Sussex to Scotland, whilst his father, Gordon, was one of the first to buy up and renovate old engines in the early '50s when they were being cut up for scrap.

After an engineering apprenticeship Michael joined his father in what is now one of the few remaining steam engineering companies in the country. Using some modern methods, such as welding as opposed to riveting, the Luggs still adhere to basic steam principles, and the 1926 Burrell was restored to its former glory using many of the same kind of tools which would have been used to make it.

In 1965 the engine was in such a state of dilapidation that its new owner was able to stick his arm right through the boiler. And for the next four years Michael Lugg gave every moment of his spare time to rebuilding it. Each evening he finished work at 7 p.m., had supper, then worked on 'William II' till past midnight.

Fortunately Michael managed to obtain the last steering worm and gear wheel left at the Thetford Works, but any other new part that was needed he had to make himself. He built up and remachined the front axle, main bearings and drive gears, as well as fitting new front bushes in the wheels, new piston rod and rubbing pads

for the crosshead and new big-end brasses. A new smoke-box and chimney were made. The inside of the coal tender was fibre-glassed to prevent rust and new copper pipes fitted.

As the rust was rubbed down the original colours emerged – green body with black, red and yellow lining, and chocolate wheels with red and ochre lines (alternative Burrell colours are maroon and red).

All four wheels are covered with tyres off Army surplus tanks. Bought in bulk, the tyres are flattened out and joined together to go round the wheel's massive perimeter. At one recent rally Michael met an ex-tank driver who had recognised the tyres on the Burrell as belonging to an American Sherman tank of the kind he had himself driven during the Second World War.

'William II' made its first appearance at a rally in 1969 at Liphook, Hants. where it won the cup for the best turned out engine. Michael won the same title at Polegate, Sussex, last year, and again this year at Frensham.

To enable him to travel back from rallies in the dark under his own steam Michael has provided a 24 watt electric light by fitting a steam generator under the engine. Steaming between 8–10 mph he travels some 400 miles a year.

Michael Lugg has been offered thousands of pounds for 'William II', but says "I'd have to be bankrupt before parting with it". His devotion to the engine has been proved on many occasions, not least in November last year, when the newly-married Mr and Mrs Michael Lugg drove away from the church in style – on the Burrell.

PLOUGHS: TURN-WREST, 1860; MAN-AND-WIFE 1900; RANSOMES STEEL-FRAME AND BALANCE PLOUGHS 1920

GENERAL SPECIFICATION

	TURN-WREST	MAN-AND-WIFE	STEEL-FRAME	BALANCE
MAKER	local	local	Ransomes	Ransomes
DATE	1860 (approx.)	1900 (approx.)	1920	1920
PLACE OF ORIGIN	S. W. Lancs.	S. W. Lancs.	Ipswich, Suffolk	Ipswich, Suffolk
BEAM	$50\frac{5}{8}''$	$30\frac{3}{4}''$	60″	35″
HANDLES	51″	42″	68″	30″
*BREAST	14″	$17\frac{1}{2}''$	16″	16″
SHARE	14″	$4\frac{3}{4}''$	$7\frac{3}{8}''$	6″
WHEELS	—	—	—	$20\frac{1}{2}''$
HEIGHT UNDER BEAM AT SHARE	$15\frac{1}{2}''$	11″	$17\frac{3}{8}''$	$18\frac{1}{2}''$
WIDTH OF SHARE	8″	3″	$7\frac{3}{4}''$	6″
LENGTH OVERALL	86″	$59\frac{3}{4}''$	131″	86″
WIDTH OVERALL	$29\frac{3}{4}''$ (over handles)	$16\frac{1}{2}''$	24″	30″ (over wheels)
TYPE OF SOIL	moss land	light	any	any

*In all cases 'Breast' is width of mould-board or boards

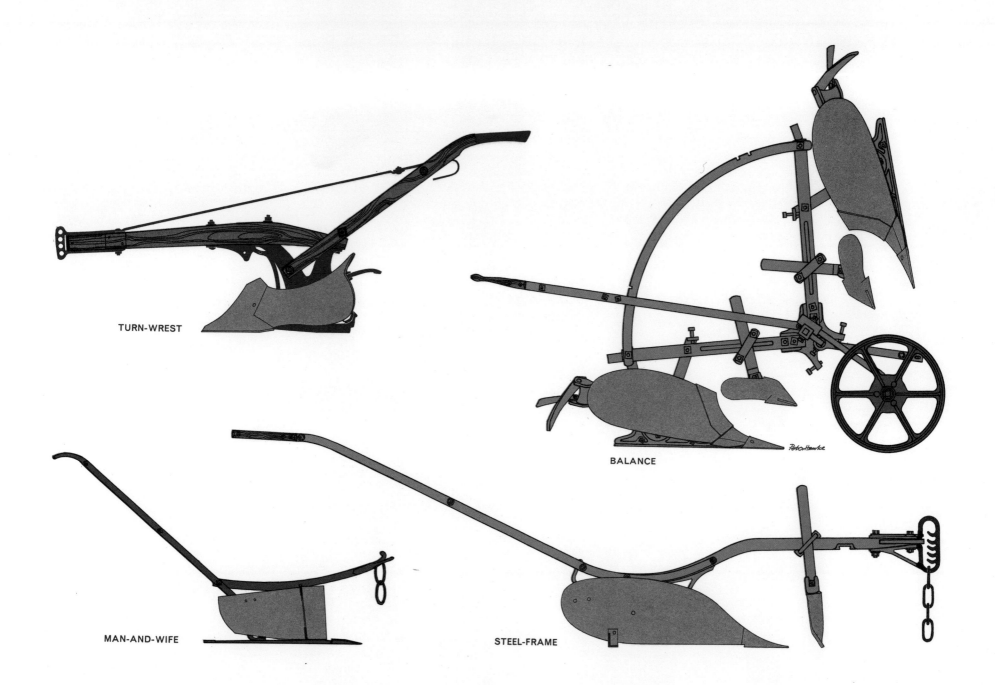

TURN-WREST

BALANCE

MAN-AND-WIFE

STEEL-FRAME

PLOUGHS: TURN-WREST, 1860; MAN-AND-WIFE 1900; RANSOMES STEEL-FRAME AND BALANCE PLOUGHS 1920

From the earliest times man has thought it necessary to stir the earth before putting in seed. The first ploughs, rough-hewn from branches, were little more than digging sticks, but both ancient writings and Egyptian monuments depict men and women tilling the ground with more sophisticated implements.

The action of a plough is a simple one. A vertical blade (or coulter) cuts through a section of soil as the point of the share makes a horizontal slice, thus cutting out a piece of earth. This slice is then turned over by a board (called the mould-board) to leave regular furrows.

No one country can be said to have invented the plough. Records show that it simply evolved all over the world in much the same way at much the same time.

By the Saxon period in England, the plough contained many of the characteristics of its modern counterpart: handles to guide; a beam to draw; coulter; share, and mould-board. With a few refinements this type of plough continued throughout the Middle Ages and, in fact, there were few changes until the eighteenth century.

Very early methods of ploughing before the mould-board, involved the ploughman tilting the plough in whatever direction he wished the furrow to lie. Although hard work it did mean that he could always turn the plough to the same point of the compass no matter what direction he was walking.

But the introduction of the fixed mould-board, although taking away much of the labour, meant that a rigid pattern of ploughing ensued. For now the slice was always thrown to the same side regardless of direction. When ploughing one way across a field the driver walked with his animals on the right-hand, with the board fixed to throw to the right so as not to impede his passage. And even when ploughing back across the field, the plough still threw to the right, making an awkward pattern of ridge and furrow.

This medieval method of ploughing was superseded in many areas by the one-way plough. This type of plough was blessed with a movable mould-board which could be fixed to turn the slice to the right when going across the field in one direction, and to the left when returning. The first one-way plough was known as the Kent plough, after the county in which it was introduced, and records of its use date back to the 1500s. A more general name for all ploughs of this kind was the turn-wrest plough, dating from the time when the ploughmen referred to mould-boards as groundwrests.

The plough on the top left of the illustration is a turn-wrest, at least 100 years old. As was customary at this time the frame was made by a local smith, the mould-board bearing the name Cockshot. This particular plough is part of the collection of Jack Johnson of Banks, Southport, Lancs. Jack, who comes from four generations of agricultural contractors, and himself worked with steam ploughing and threshing tackle, has built up a varied collection of agricultural implements during the past three years.

An avowed steam man – his steam 'parties' have raised thousands of pounds for charity – Jack Johnson spends most of his spare time restoring traction engines and any other farm machinery that comes his way. His work brings him into contact with many examples of exciting old implements, often discovered quite by chance. This was the case with the turn-wrest plough which was found amongst a jumble of other ploughs in a barn belonging to an old farmer. Known locally as a 'turn-over' plough, its antiquity is betrayed by the wooden beam, as iron frames were not common till the nineteenth century.

Although by no means comprehensive, Jack Johnson's collection of ploughs gives a sure indication of the way in which this indispensable implement developed. One of his most intriguing examples is known as a man-and-wife plough.

Small-holders, too poor to own a horse, had to provide their own power as best they could. In this case the husband was in harness pulling the plough, whilst his wife steered. On some models the handles can be reversed, and the ploughman walked backwards dragging his plough. (See illustration bottom left).

The steel-framed plough on the bottom right of the illustration was produced by the prolific company of Ransomes around 1920. The end of the nineteenth century and the beginning of the present was a time of change, when factories began turning out many different types of ploughs, suited to different tasks on different soils.

A wheel-less plough, this is known as a swing plough. Wheels on ploughs are, in fact, a fairly modern invention to prevent the beam from going too deep in the ground, or from rising too quickly out. The swing plough has long handles to give the ploughman good leverage and a short beam to limit the leverage of the horses. By contrast a wheeled plough gave the plough-man less work so has short handles and a longer beam to accommodate the wheels.

This steel-frame plough was mainly used for work in the autumn, shown by the long plate and share which enabled the slice to turn over without crumbling. The previously buried surface was then exposed to the air. In contrast a spring plough is characterised by a short, digging share as the soil needed a different kind of treatment at the beginning of the year.

Jack Johnson's swing plough was, like many others, given to him by a farmer friend. Many curious visitors to his collection often exclaim that they have even older pieces at home which he may have. Although much is worthless from a historical point of view there is usually one implement of interest amongst a cart-load.

Another plough which he gained in this way is the graceful looking balance plough shown on the top right of the illustration. Another nineteenth century plough, this model was horse-drawn, although balance ploughs were also made to be driven by steam. It consists of two complete share/mouldboard units mounted (but facing in opposite directions) on an arc-shaped beam, which can be thrown over to reverse the plough. At the end of the furrow the horse is turned, dragging the harness chain underneath the wheels and, at the same time, the ploughman throws over the arc beam so bringing into use the other share/mouldboard unit.

Commonly called a butterfly plough because of its shape, this particular plough is given different names in different parts of the country.

Jack Johnson knows it as a half-moon plough, but in Devon, it is called by the more prosaic name of a cock-up.

Ploughs, dairy machinery, old carts and wagons form a major part of Jack Johnson's collection, though pride of place must go to his traction engines. He remembers meeting with scant response in sceptical Lancashire when he bought his first engine for restoration. And many were the cynics who refused to "pay 2s just to look at a load of old scrap" when he first opened his barn to the public. However, when word got around of the magnificent sight of the big engines in steam and the other weird implements on show, people began to pour in.

For Jack Johnson and his friends, reward for their hours of labour – over 30 hours a week – comes from seeing children's faces as their grandfathers explain the workings of these old machines to them. As the youngsters learn, so the old men have their memories. Often, ex-ploughmen ask just to be able to hold the ploughs. "You can see them going back 30 years" says Jack Johnson delightedly, "remembering all those hours behind the horses, which makes me feel it is all the more worthwhile".

FOWLER PLOUGHING ENGINE, No. 14727, 1918, "PEACE"
WITH FIVE FURROW BALANCE PLOUGH

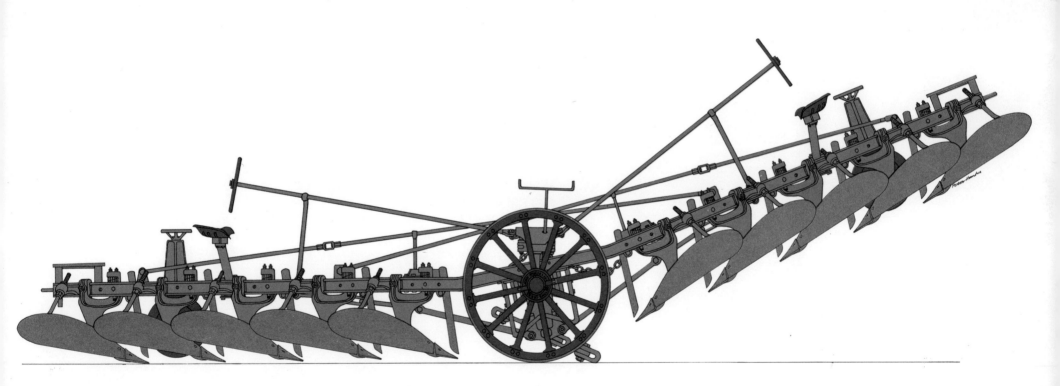

FOWLER PLOUGHING ENGINE, No. 14727, 1918, "PEACE"

Without doubt the best known name in steam cultivation is that of John Fowler of Leeds. Born in the West country in 1826, Fowler first attracted attention with his mole drainer, a type of plough specially suited to wet ground. As the bullet-shaped mole, attached to the plough's vertical blade, was carried through the earth it made a channel which acted as a drainpipe: the top soil was then automatically covered over.

In 1856 Fowler produced his first balance plough which remained virtually unchanged for the next 80 years (see illustration page 25). At first unsuccessful, in that his machines, although as effective as horse ploughs, were considered less economical, Fowler eventually carried off the prize for the most efficient method of ploughing at the Chester Royal Show in 1858. With this success behind him he set up his own works at Leeds, only to have his career tragically curtailed just three years later when he was killed in a hunting accident.

Shortly before his death Fowler exhibited the ploughing method for which he is most remembered: two steam engines standing at opposite sides of a field winch the plough, cultivator or mole drainer backwards and forwards between them. He would be pleased indeed to know that nearly 100 years later a pair of his engines are still in use on an Essex farm. For Harold Jackson of Thurstons Farm,

Toppesfield, having ploughed with steam all his life, like his father before him, firmly contends that it is still the best way of cultivating the heavy East Anglian soil.

Purchased new in 1918 by his father at a cost of £5,250, the pair of Fowler engines, numbers 14726 and 7, came complete with plough, cultivator, mole drainer, water cart and living van on a special train from the Leeds factory. They arrived at Thurstons farm on November 11, Armistice Day and were named 'Peace' and 'Victory'.

Until the advent of the internal combustion engine which made tractors available to many of the smaller farmers, the Fowlers and their tackle were hired out on contracting work. Travelling from farm to farm for most of the year, 'Peace' and 'Victory' were only taken inside in January and February for repairs. On the road a six-man team was needed to handle all the equipment: one to drive each engine, one for the cultivator, two for the plough, and a cook boy. Starting work at 15, the boy would progress up through handling the plough, to driving the big engines at around 18 years old.

A typical day's labour would begin at 4 a.m. and not end till 9 or 10 p.m. Sleep was at a premium, the men tumbling for a few hours rest into bunks in the living van, their home for most

of the year. Sadly, of all the original machinery, only the living van is no longer in Mr Jackson's possession: it was purchased by the Church Army as quarters for evacuees during the Second World War.

During the summer, when sticky tar on the roads made day-time travelling an impossibility for the 20-ton engines, they had to restrict their movements to the late evening. Harold Jackson laughingly tells of the time when, steaming at midnight down a country lane, 'Peace' disturbed a local resident, an old Colonel, by shaking the pictures from the walls of his house as she passed. Dashing out into the road in his night attire the Colonel remonstrated with the driver before retiring angrily to bed.

Imagine his astonishment when, just ten minutes later, 'Victory' – alike in every detail to her sister engine – caused exactly the same disturbance. And imagine the bewilderment of the second driver who, oblivious of the first incident, was also loudly harangued for having the nerve to drive up and down the same road when he had already been warned!

The two engines, size A A7 – the largest to come out of the Fowler works – are indeed impressive. When working they burned one ton of coal per engine, per day, imbibing 200 gallons of water an acre. The original water cart, still in use, though now pulled by tractor instead of horses, holds 225 gallons. Natural brook water only is used as it contains no impurities which might damage the boilers.

This same concern for detail and preservation of what is good is mirrored in the rest of Harold Jackson's farming. His corn, brought in from the fields on 100-year-old Essex wagons, is still threshed by an 1898 drum which he swears is more effective than noisy combines. Although tractors are used to power the belt which works the drum, Mr Jackson reiterates that "there's something about steam that the combustion engine will never replace, the smell of the smoke, the sense of enormous power and the satisfaction of a job well done".

Author C. H. Warren, who spent a harvest with the Jacksons at Thurstons during the war, when writing *The Land is Yours**, echoes this same sentiment in his book, describing 'Peace' and 'Victory' at work: "When those two engines are going full-steam, one on this headland, one on that, and the mighty plough is being hauled steadily between them, I know of nothing in all the farming year that can thrill me more. Here indeed, man has harnessed power for the good – and nothing but the good – of the land".

* Eyre and Spottiswoode Ltd.

GENERAL SPECIFICATION

MAKER	John Fowler & Co.
DATE	1918
PLACE OF ORIGIN	Leeds, Yorks.
MACHINE TYPE	Winch Ploughing Engine
CYLINDER TYPE	Compound
N.H.P.	18
CYLINDER DIMENSIONS	7″ × 12″
BOILER DIMENSION	2′ 9¾″
LENGTH OVERALL	23′ 5½″
WIDTH OVERALL	8′ 9½″
WEIGHT	17 ton 18 cwt.
REAR WHEELS	6′ 6″ × 24″
FRONT WHEELS	5′ ½″ × 18″
VALVE GEAR	Firth

RANSOMES THRESHING DRUM, NO. 59112, 1935

GENERAL SPECIFICATION

MAKER	Ransomes, Sims and Jefferies
DATE	1935 (approx).
PLACE OF ORIGIN	Ipswich, Suffolk
MACHINE TYPE	A 54
N.H.P.	6–8
B.H.P.	28
WIDTH OF DRUM	4' 6"
DIAMETER OF DRUM	22"
REVS. PER MINUTE	1050
LENGTH	21'
WIDTH	8'
WEIGHT	103 cwt.
HEIGHT TO PLATFORM	9'
APPROX. QUANTITY OF WHEAT PER HOUR	55–90 bushels
APPROX. QUANTITY OF BARLEY PER HOUR	65–105 bushels
APPROX. QUANTITY OF OATS PER HOUR	85–145 bushels

Peter Hauke

30

Whatever nineteenth century agricultural engineers lacked in resources they more than made up for in team spirit, struggling inventors and reputable companies banding together to introduce startling new machinery. The young John Fowler, for example, at first without capital to implement his ideas, wisely enlisted the aid of the already-established Ipswich engineering firm of Ransomes, Sims and Jefferies who produced his revolutionary balance plough (see page 25).

Founded in 1789 with just £200 and only two employees, today Ransomes employs over 3,000 workers and exports throughout the world. The company, manufacturers of the world's very first lawn mowing machine, was also the first to win the Royal Agricultural Society's gold medal, presented for its exhibits at the Oxford Show in 1839.

In 1841 Ransomes exhibited the first ever portable steam threshing machine, and the following year won a prize with this machine which would cope with wheat, barley, oats, rye, etc. Ransome's threshing drums, with their distinctive orange and red colouring were to be found in farm yards throughout the country for nearly a century. Powered first by steam engines – both portable and traction – then later by tractors, these drums were to provide a vital service until made redundant with the arrival

of the multi-purpose combines in the 1940s.

Although an early threshing machine was produced as early as 1636, flailing the grain to separate it from the chaff, and thus render it marketable to miller or corn merchant, was generally a hand operation until well into the eighteenth century. A back-breaking task, it was at least regarded as a companionable one, as up to ten men at a time worked their way across the barn beating away at the crop with sticks.

The advent of the fast and efficient threshing drum changed all that, as the noise and speed of working made conversation virtually impossible. In general, threshing by this method was regarded as a necessary evil, and many of today's farmers who worked on the drums have eyesight permanently scarred from the constant battering of whirling grain.

Also, like general purpose engines and steam ploughing tackle, the drums were beyond the pockets of most small farmers who had to rely on contractors. With a large area to cover and many farms to visit, the contracting team often lost valuable time through wet weather, so that each farmer had to be prepared to accommodate them whenever they turned up, no matter what other activity he was then engaged in.

However, when once the threshing tackle

arrived all was frenzied motion. The sheaves were first forked from the stack onto the top of the thresher, where there were one or two men cutting the strings or bands round the sheaves. The latter were then handed to another man who fed them into the drum. The crop was rubbed between beaters on a revolving drum and the bars of the concave, the grain dropping through the concave onto the shoe fitted with sieves whilst the straw passed onto the shakers for any further separation. Any light material such as chaff which went through with the grain was separated by means of air blowers which blew it out of the side of the machine whilst the grain was delivered to the back end of the thresher and sacked off. The straw moved along the shakers and was passed out at the front end.

Although a comparatively recent product of the Ransomes' works, in that it was made around 1935, drum no. 59112, still embodies the same principles of design as those made by the company at the end of the nineteenth century. Owned now by Alan Troop, a Lincolnshire arable farmer, this particular model was in use only 15 years ago, and is still in full working order.

A collector of old farm machinery for the past ten years, Mr. Troop purchased his threshing drum some three years ago from a neighbouring farmer to save it from being chopped up for firewood. He admits to liking such machines as a reaction against today's push-button methods of agriculture. And, looking round his farm, where huge, impersonal silos and hangar-like buildings dominate the landscape, it is easy to believe with him that "complete mechanisation has taken the enthusiasm out of modern farming".

Alan Troop's own particular enthusiasm is directed mainly towards stationary agricultural engines. Structurally less imposing than the more showy traction engines, less powerful than the portables, these fixed steam, petrol or paraffin engines were nevertheless within the reach of the small farmer and, as such played a vital part in the development of British agriculture. Used to power lighting plants, water systems, saw benches and milking machines along with other barn machinery these engines were mainly of American make, although many British companies also produced them. Amongst Alan Troop's collection of engines is an 1890 Robey steam engine, an 1895 'Victoria' paraffin engine with blow lamp start and a similar type made by Hornsby of Grantham in 1902.

Stationary engines are becoming popular with collectors today as there are still quite a few of them to be found disused in barns and factories, and consequently they are relatively inexpensive. Even mechanically-minded teenagers, as yet unable to afford their own cars, gain great pleasure from restoring these models to working order.

Alan Troop's own interest also extends to scale models. Known throughout the district as an engine buff he is always being told of any likely purchases. But perhaps his greatest 'find' was the original working specifications for a Robey portable which he is adapting to create a three-inch scale model complete with copper boiler. Now that the Lincolnshire engineering firm has closed down Mr. Troop feels that he is providing his own working memorial to it and some of the engines which bore the once-proud name of Robey.

GLASGOW TRACTOR, NO. 110, 1918

GENERAL SPECIFICATION

MAKER	Wallace (Glasgow) Ltd.
DATE	1918
PLACE OF ORIGIN	Glasgow
MACHINE TYPE	Motor tractor
B.H.P.	Developing 27 at 850 r.p.m.
LENGTH OVERALL	11' 4"
WIDTH OVERALL	5'
WEIGHT	$37\frac{1}{2}$ cwt.
WHEELS	39" diameter
WHEELBASE	75"
GROUND CLEARANCE	14"
CYLINDER TYPE	4-cylinder
WATER TANK CAPACITY	8 gallons (inc. radiator)
FUEL	Paraffin
GOVERNOR TYPE	Pickering
BRAKE TYPE	Cast-iron pedal-operated
CLUTCH	Steel cone type
BELT SPEED	2,600' per min.
AVERAGE SPEEDS	$2\frac{1}{2}$ mph (low), $4\frac{1}{2}$ mph (high), $2\frac{3}{4}$ mph (reverse)

If ever a machine can be said to have been born of necessity it is the internal combustion engined tractor for use in British agriculture. Tractors – the word was little used until around 1906 – were first produced in the United States at the end of the nineteenth century. Still looking like steam traction engines they made no impact on English farming at this time.

By 1902 however, Dan Albone, a young engineer from Biggleswade, Beds. had produced his first British tractor, the Ivel (the original is now in the Science Museum, London), and his Company continued to manufacture about 90 of this model until hit by the depression in the 1920s. Yet few other engineering companies in this country gave much thought to the development of motor tractors, so that the use of steam continued virtually unchecked till the beginning of the First World War.

Then came the big leap forward. The supreme effectiveness of the German submarine blockade finally awakened the British people to the fact that, in order to survive, we had to be capable of producing all our own food, a task made increasingly difficult by the lack of able-bodied men and horses. So, in an attempt to plough up and sow some three million acres of grassland in the fastest possible time, the Government imported every motor tractor available, a few European but mostly American.

There were obvious initial difficulties, for qualified engineers were in short supply and experienced operators all the more so. Spares and repairs were not easy to come by, but were often needed, as many of the ploughing attachments were unsuited to certain types of British soil. So urgent was the need however, that farmers were forced to adapt to the new methods, and by the end of the war the internal combustion engine had won a place for itself on the English landscape.

This was a time for reappraisal. By now there were over 180 tractor manufacturers and many farmers, ignorant of the particular attributes of each machine, were at a loss to know which type to purchase. So, in 1919 the Royal Agricultural Society in conjunction with the Society of Motor Manufacturers and Traders held tractor trials at South Carlton, Lincs. Amongst 30 makes of tractors entered was a Scottish built Glasgow, manufactured by Wallace (Glasgow) Ltd. in 1918, at a cost of £450. A three-wheel tractor, it was ahead of its time in that all the wheels were driven, the four-cylinder 27 hp engine transmitting power to the rear wheel by a bevel pinion and spur wheels. When travelling on a straight course all three wheels drive as though solidly connected. The arrangement is such that, when turning, the front wheel which is on the inner track, describes the same path as the rear wheel, and the outer wheel is enabled to overrun by its ratchet gear.

Very few of these tractors were ever produced, and only two still exist. The one shown in the print, no. 110, is owned – along with some 60 others – by John Moffitt of Peepy Farm, Stocksfield, Northumberland, who has perhaps the greatest collection of vintage tractors in the country.

Moffitt, a dairy and arable farmer with some 1,500 acres and three farms to supervise, first became interested in preserving early agricultural machinery some eight years ago. His first purchase was an American Oliver, made in 1942 and shipped here at the end of the Second World War. Designed primarily for rowcrop work it is of an advanced design.

During the next few years the Moffitt collection grew so large that the question of adequate accommodation became a pressing problem. Then, having taken over a nearby property at West Side, Newton, Mr Moffitt decided that as the buildings were incapable of modernisation he would convert them into a permanent home for his machines.

The West Side 'old crocks' hospital' has been

much publicised, and many farmers are pleased to let John Moffitt give their early machines a final resting place. Up to 500 hours can be spent restoring rusty wrecks to immaculate working condition.

Last year some 1,200 visitors saw the collection and John Moffitt admits that it has now grown so large that he is no longer able to put in all the time he would wish. To turn West Side into a true museum of rural life Mr Moffitt has acquired a complete blacksmith's shop with anvil, horse-shoes and tools. In the domestic section there is a selection of ancient pots and pans, kettles, flat irons and a copper steam bath. Outside in the yard are ranged unusual stack stands, always made round and smooth to prevent vermin from climbing up and eating the corn.

But John Moffitt admits that his first love is, and always will be, tractors. Amongst many beautifully restored engines in his collection are 22 models produced before 1920 including a 1917 'Weeks', one of only a very small number built, and the only one left in existence; a 1929 Allis Chalmers, Model U, the first tractor to have rubber tyres as standard equipment; a 1914 Mogul, the first type of tractor made by the American International Harvester Company ever to be exported to this country; a 1919 British Wallis made by Ruston, Hornsby Ltd. of

Lincoln, now the only one left in the country; and a U.S. Wallis Cub Junior with three wheels, one of the first frameless tractors ever made.

Fordsons, the agricultural brainchild of motoring genius Henry Ford, have a prominent place in the Moffitt collection. The first Ford tractor appeared in 1907, and by 1920, with added refinements, had sold some 100,000 models; 6,000 being imported into England during the First World War.

The Fordson's main advantage was that it was the first ever tractor to integrate the engine and body as one power unit. Previous tractors were simply clumsy iron frames with four wheels and the engine bolted on. The Fordson was ten years ahead of its time, so much so in fact, that it gradually drove most other makes off the market, and by 1930 only 38 tractor manufacturers remained.

One such manufacturer was Harry Ferguson, one-time Ford employee and inventor of the three-point linkage system which enabled tractors to carry other implements above the soil's surface. In a successful suit, Ferguson sued Ford for incorporating this device in their tractors, and received over £3½ million in compensation.

Today's tractors still bear striking resemblance to Henry Ford's 1916 design. Yet how different they are from the majority of the collection found at West Side. And tomorrow's generation of children will continue to be thankful to men like John Moffitt for preserving these ancient tractors for their education and delight.

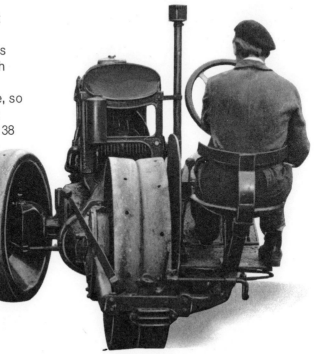

TASKER "BOAT" WAGON, 1901

GENERAL SPECIFICATION

MAKER	Taskers
DATE	1901
PLACE OF ORIGIN	Andover, Hants.
WAGON STYLE	Dorsetshire
SIZE	Standard
LENGTH OVERALL	11' 6"
WIDTH OVERALL	5' 11"
BRAKE TYPE	Drug shoe and chain
AXLE SIZE	$2\frac{1}{4}$"
CAPACITY	$2\frac{1}{2}$ tons
PRICE WHEN NEW	£30

TASKER "BOAT" WAGON, 1901

Man's best friend in the days before steam locomotion was undoubtedly the horse on whom he depended for the major part of his motive power. Even when most horse-driven pieces of machinery were replaced by other forms of power, the horse was still valuable between the shafts of a wagon or cart, servicing the more unwieldy steam engines at harvest time.

Wagons–thought to have been first introduced into Britain in the sixteenth century – were the result of months of exacting labour by village craftsmen. Each elegant curve had a practical value. As any excess weight would add to the horse's burden, chamfering – shaving away unnecessary timber – played some part in producing efficient as well as attractive vehicles.

Most wagons had a common type of under-carriage but different body shapes which varied according to geographical location. The size of the wheels also varied in different parts of the country. Each wheel, dish-shaped in that the spokes were set in a different place from the rim and hub to prevent breakage when the wagon swayed from side to side, was in itself a masterpiece of construction.

The two main types of wagons up to the early nineteenth century were the Box Wagon (variations on a basic box shape) and the Hoop-raved or Bow Wagon (the side timbers curving elegantly over the back wheel). Wagons varied enormously within these two categories, each county type being built to take into account the vagaries of the terrain. So, a typical Yorkshire wagon for use on rugged ground, would be heavier than one used on the light soil of the southern counties. This also would vary in some details depending whether it was meant for work in the soft Yorkshire Dales or on the harsher moors.

The colour of wagons also depended on local preferences. Bodies were usually painted blue or yellow with red wheels and undercarriage, but again this was a matter of custom, some colours being thought unlucky in certain places.

Although wagons continued to be hand-built till the end of the nineteenth century they were gradually replaced by factory-made products. As with other aspects of farming, economy of function took over from elegance of design, and the demand began to be for speedily manufactured, efficient wagons. As early as 1864 cast iron began to be used for wheel hubs instead of elm, and eventually more and more iron was employed to strengthen the basic structure. Based on the old patterns, factory wagons saved both time and money, so that the art of the local wheelwright eventually began to die out.

The most popular type of factory-made wagon was the 'boat' shape in which the side-boards were made from two planks sloping outwards like a ship's hull. This became a popular alternative to the hoop-rave wagon, the upper board serving as the lade or overhanging shelf which increased the carrying capacity and prevented the load from dropping onto the wheels.

The first 'boat' wagon was patented by the Hampshire engineering company, Taskers of Andover, to add one more popular product to their vast range of agricultural and commercial machinery. Taskers' output was phenomenal for over 100 years – the firm is still in existence – especially for a rural-based concern which started from humble beginnings.

The founder of the company, Robert Tasker, a Wiltshire blacksmith, travelled into Hampshire in 1806 in search of work. Employed by the village blacksmith of Abbotts Ann, Robert eventually took over the business and became so successful that his brother William joined him. In 1813 they opened the foundry which was to be the base of the most prolific engineering company in the country.

Named Waterloo Ironworks after Britain's famous victory, the Taskers' foundry turned out ploughs, well-heads, mile-stones, iron signs, porches and even bridges. Later Taskers seized eagerly on the boom in steam traction engines, concentrating on road haulage rather than agricultural uses. Their Little Giant tractors hit the market at exactly the right time. Each engine was supplied with two trailers to ensure maximum efficiency, and it was on similar trailers that Taskers consolidated their reputation.

During the Second World War Taskers, now controlled by the Fuller family, were under contract to the War Department to supply aircraft-recovery vehicles. The prototype of this trailer, known as the Queen Mary, was produced within ten days of receiving working drawings, and in all nearly 4,000 were produced. Such was the shortage of aircraft, that Taskers, with their invaluable trailer, can be said to have played a considerable part in helping win the Battle of Britain.

After the war, the Fullers established a Tasker Museum within the works, containing fine examples of much old machinery and iron-ware produced by the company in its long history. Unfortunately when the firm was once again taken over it was deemed necessary to clear out the exhibits so that space could be more profitably used, and the collection was put up for sale. It seemed as if the items were doomed to find separate homes.

At the eleventh hour a group of local people interested in preserving the Tasker machines came together to form a Trust which managed to buy many of the most interesting pieces in the collection. These are now housed by the Hampshire County Museum Service but are not yet on public view.

Amongst many fine items in the collection is the Dorsetshire pattern 'boat' wagon pictured on the previous page. Built by Taskers in 1901 the wagon is more standardised than earlier craftsmen-made ones, but still has a graceful line. First painted dark blue it is now black with red undercarriage.

When the wagon was used for harvesting, special ladders would be attached through eyes in the floor-boards to contain the high load. Such a wagon has a capacity of two-and-a-half tons, and this one was still bringing in the harvest in 1963 without any visible signs of wear. It is fitted with a type of brake known as a drug shoe, a cast iron wedge chained to the hindwheel to lessen the speed when going downhill, the wear being taken by the wedge rather than the tyre.

Wagons, ploughs, a winnowing machine, steam portable and traction engines, even an old painted sign for the Anna Valley Speedwell, the Taskers' coffee house, are part of the

unique collection now under the care of the Tasker Trust. There is no similar collection of machinery made by one company over such a period of time in the country. It is to be hoped that very soon these outstanding old machines will be given the home they deserve.

GARRETT SUFFOLK PUNCH, NO. 33180, 1919, "THE JOKER"

GENERAL SPECIFICATION

MAKER	Richard Garrett & Sons
DATE	1919
PLACE OF ORIGIN	Leiston, Suffolk
MACHINE TYPE	Agrimotor
N.H.P.	4
B.H.P.	35
CYLINDER DIMENSIONS	4" 7"
LENGTH OVERALL	14' 7"
WIDTH OVERALL	7' 6"
WEIGHT	5 tons
WORKING PRESSURE	220 lbs
WATER TANK CAPACITY	185 gallons
GOVERNOR TYPE	Pickering
DRIVE ARRANGEMENT	2" roller chain
BRAKE TYPE	Band on rear wheel
VALVE GEAR	Piston valve
AVERAGE SPEED	8 mph

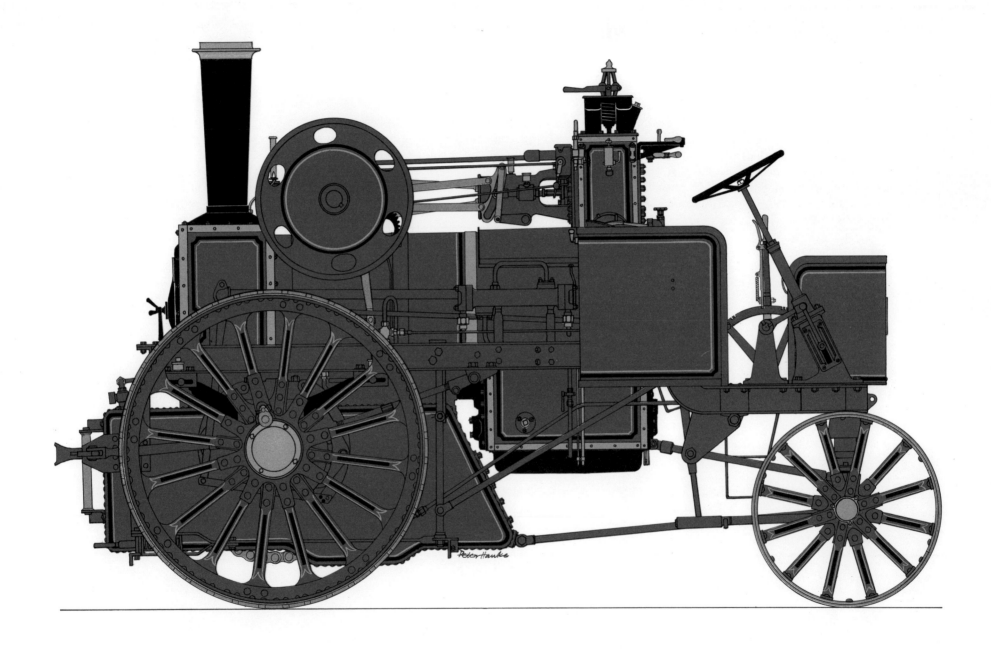

GARRETT SUFFOLK PUNCH, NO. 33180, 1919, "THE JOKER"

Steam engineering may have been killed by the advent of the internal combustion engine, but it refused to die without a struggle. When the urgent need for speed during the First World War forced the heavy steam machines off the land to be replaced by lighter, quicker, paraffin-engined tractors, some steam engineers turned their talents to producing rival fast, easily handled traction engines.

Such was the case with Richard Garrett & Sons of Leiston Works, Suffolk. Founded in 1778, the company produced many excellent types of steam engines before being amalgamated, and eventually forming the electrical business which still exists today.

In 1919, in an effort to combat the motor tractor, Garretts produced a light, 4 nhp steam tractor known as the Suffolk Punch. This remarkable little engine was intended to show that steam ploughing was not only the prerogative of the big league, the huge winch ploughing engines (see page 24), but could be achieved successfully with the plough pulled directly behind the engine, in exactly the same way as the internal combustion engined tractor.

Of apparent revolutionary design in that the engine appeared to be going backwards with the chimney at the rear and the steering controls at the front, the Suffolk Punch was, in fact, simply the common Garrett traction engine in reverse. Unfortunately, at the time few realised this. People liked their steam engines to look like conventional steam engines, and so the Suffolk Punch was never the success it really deserved to be.

Four engines of this type were built for trials and proved both quick and light, being chain driven with motor car type controls. Yet they were too late. For few wanted a five-ton tractor with all the complications of raising steam when they could buy a 16–17 cwt. Fordson motor tractor. Eventually all but two of Garrett's Suffolk Punches were broken up for scrap.

Luckily, therefore, an example of this fine engine still remains today in an excellent state of preservation. Named 'The Joker', engine no. 33180 was first purchased by a farmer in Kent where it spent most of its working life. Later a Mr. Lambert took it over for use in Norfolk and Suffolk, and it was then sold to Giles Romanes, President of the Dorset Steam and Historic Vehicle Club. For some time the Suffolk Punch stood in a yard in Maidenhead in a derelict condition until being rescued by its present owner, Jim Hutchins of Wimborne, Dorset.

When found the engine's chassis was twisted and badly corroded so that a completely new chassis had to be built. A new smoke box was made, as well as a new coal tender and a complete new floor and apron. The motion was also completely dismantled and rebuilt. The most difficult job was to replace the chimney. Mr. Hutchins had no idea of the original length and, as no one could advise him on this, spent some five years of trial and error before arriving at the correct answer.

Repairs were carried out to the boiler plate and the boiler itself retubed. The front axle was straightened and re-machined and the front wheels re-bushed. Similarly the rear wheels were bored out and new bushes made and the rear springs were re-set.

'The Joker' was finally repainted in its original green and black colours, taken from traces of the existing paint found in un-exposed places.

Jim Hutchins, born as he says "virtually with a coal shovel in my hand" hails originally from Nottinghamshire where his father was a steam haulage contractor, but has spent most of his life in the South West, and now has the largest collection of engines in that part of the world. He began buying up old engines in the 1950s to save them from the breakers' yards, and soon amassed around 30 of all types. At that time he intended to start a steam museum but the local authority frowned on the venture which had to be scrapped.

Nothing daunted, Jim Hutchins kept on collecting and restoring engines. Sensibly realising that he himself could only drive one at a time he sold many of the engines at low prices to other enthusiasts who, he was confident, would also preserve them.

Many other young people, unable to actually buy engines, owe much to Jim Hutchins. For Jim provides all the equipment and facilities for restoring the old 'steamers' whilst his young friends provide most of the labour. "I am fully recompensed by the work they put in" he says, "and the resulting entertainment it gives to thousands of people."

Sometimes, Mr Hutchins admits, he barely hears of his engines more than once or twice a year when a young 'owner' phones with a query. These engines are more or less on permanent loan to those who have restored them, being shown at rallies throughout the country.

Although he finished with steam haulage in 1929 Jim Hutchins is today recognised as one of the ultimate authorities in the steam world on Sentinel wagons. He may preserve agricultural engines but his heart lies with the tough little steam lorries, forerunners of modern heavy haulage vehicles. Five Sentinels still remain in his yard, and one of them is often to be seen

hauling a low-loader containing the Suffolk Punch to a rally.

Like many of the leading steam owners Mr Hutchins travels hundreds of miles a year with his engines for charity, from as far West as Cornwall to Chester-le-Street, Co. Durham in the North, taking in Birmingham, Leeds and Harrogate on the way. Over the past 15 years he estimates that, in all, rallies in which he has taken part have provided some £18,000 for various charities.

Up to a few years ago Jim's wife Connie used to do the firing for him as they steamed some 4,000 miles a year. Nowadays she is content, for health reasons, with a more passive role, although she never misses a steam event, and enjoys entertaining their many friends in their travelling caravan. Mr and Mrs Hutchins also have a portable steam railway which they take around to spastic children at nine homes on the south coast.

Many people throughout the country have cause to be thankful for Jim Hutchins' great interest in steam. They need have no fear that it will ever fade away. Says Jim: "There's something about steam . . . once you've worked with it you never lose your love for it". And he confesses that this affection for the engines is bound up with his love for humanity. For in his

experience, exactly the same makes of engine from the same manufacturer have different foibles and characteristics. As he says "steam engines are the nearest things to human beings I have ever come across!".

TITAN TRACTOR, NO. TU 7988, 1916

GENERAL SPECIFICATION

MAKER	International Harvester Company
DATE	1916
PLACE OF ORIGIN	Milwaukee, USA
MACHINE TYPE	Motor tractor
N.H.P.	10
B.H.P.	20
CYLINDER TYPE	2-cylinder
CYLINDER DIMENSIONS	$6\frac{1}{4}''$ bore, 8" stroke
LENGTH OVERALL	11' 7"
WIDTH AT FRONT	3' 3"
WIDTH AT REAR	4' 9"
WHEEL-BASE	7' 10"
WEIGHT	3 tons 1 cwt.
FUEL	Paraffin
FUEL TANK CAPACITY	16 gallons
WATER TANK CAPACITY	35 gallons
STEERING	Worm and sector
DRIVE ARRANGEMENT	4-wheel chain driven
AVERAGE SPEEDS	2 mph (low), $2\frac{3}{4}$ mph (high), 3 mph (reverse)

46

Among the dozens of different makes of motor tractors imported into this country during the First World War, few bore any resemblance to their modern counterparts, and indeed even to Henry Ford's timeless prototype, the 1916 Fordson (see page 35). In 1914 the internal combustion-engined tractor was suffering from exactly the same teething troubles as the motor car two decades previously. And, in general, tractor engineering at this time followed a swerving path between eccentricity and efficiency.

One such tractor, which served as a happy amalgam of the old and the new, was the International Harvester Company's Titan, some 3,500 of which were shipped to Britain from the Chicago-based engineering firm between 1914–1919. Looking more like a small steam traction engine than most other tractors, the Titan did not, however, sport a smoke box. Its most salient feature was a boiler-shaped water tank with a capacity of around 35 gallons. And, oddly enough there was no radiator, water simply being circulated through a pipe from the bottom of the water tank, round the cylinder and back by overhead return pipe.

The Titan's two-cylinder engine ran on paraffin but was started by petrol. About a pint of the latter fuel was needed to preheat the manifold and vaporise the paraffin. Then, as soon as the engine was ticking over, the petrol supply was shut off and the paraffin fed in from a tank which held around 16 gallons.

A needle valve enabled water to be injected into the paraffin and the resulting dilution prevented the engine from 'pinking', especially when the tractor was running under heavy load.

Ignition was by magneto, the engine being started by a handle on the fly-wheel. A separate handle was provided with all Titans, but with one of International's other early makes, the Mogul, there was no such sophistication, so that a sharp tug on the fly-wheel had to suffice as a starting device. Naturally this was pretty dangerous for inexperienced operators, and one Mogul owner, Richard Dockeray of Ashford, Kent, wrote to tell us of the occasion when his tractor reacted to clumsy starting procedures by throwing a farm labourer up in the air and breaking both his legs!

Titans, Moguls, and all other tractors with steel wheels, also became terrors of the road, as their heavy, untyred wheels – though supposedly suitable for road work – played havoc with all types of surface. Luckily for motorists, the tractors' top speed was only around 3 mph so they were prevented from doing the vast amount of damage which would have come with higher speeds.

Despite its unconventional appearance the Titan was an efficient, reliable machine which stood up well to the demands imposed upon it by war work. This is proved by the experience of the Kent war agricultural committee which worked some 15 different makes of tractor over a four-year period: at the end of the war they were left with 112 Titans, 64 Fordsons and four of another American make, the Overtime.

A heavy machine (approximately three tons) the Titan needed dry ground to operate best, and often lost valuable time during bad weather. Records of the Kent committee quoted in the Royal Agricultural Society's *Journal* for 1918 show that, during that year, on average a Titan took two-and-a-half hours to harvest an acre, including time off for breakdowns, wet weather and road travelling.

The Titan had an obvious advantage over horses on heavy land and was most effective when used for ploughing, cultivating, drawing a harrow etc. It also had an advantage over other tractors in that, fitted with a very short front axle so that the back wheels did not run in the same tracks as the front, the Titan's weight was distributed more evenly over the field, and it did not leave such heavy marks. However, this plus was partly offset by the fact that the plough and other attachments were unable to be attached directly behind the tractor which made for steering difficulties and loss of power.

That Titans were built to last throughout succeeding generations is proved, in that the one depicted in our picture was one of the original number which came over from the United States during the First World War. It is now owned by the farming Critchlow brothers of Tamworth, Staffs., whose father purchased it in 1919, from the War Executive Committee at a sale in Grantham, Lincs., for £500. Built around 1916 at International's Milwaukee works, the Titan is still in first-class working order, regularly attending local rallies in the district.

Although the tractor ceased active life as regards threshing etc., some six years ago, it is still used from time to time on timber work, and Randolph Critchlow believes that with regular care the engine could continue indefinitely. Only the magneto is not original: it was changed in 1940. And, amazingly, nothing has been spent on the tractor since the winter of 1941 when new rings were fitted on the pistons to prevent its using too much oil.

The Critchlows consider their Titan to be as effective as modern tractors, although slower and requiring more effort to drive. Yet, even so they feel the Titan to be a more economical machine to run: on a test run in 1942 when fuel

was just 10½d. per gallon the tractor worked from 8 a.m. to 5 p.m. and used only seven gallons of paraffin.

Today there is no use for the heavy Titan on the 240 acres of land owned by the Critchlows which is mainly given over to market gardening. Yet the family, whose connection with the land goes back to 1214, will continue to preserve the tractor, if only to remind themselves of how much farming has advanced in their lifetime.

The two brothers well remember playing truant from school in 1916 to get their first glimpse of the beast which was revitalising English agriculture – a Titan tractor, exact in every detail to the one they now own. And

Randolph Critchlow at the controls of the 1916 Titan tractor

although they had to pay for missing lessons, both Critchlows believe that seeing the tractor, was worth any indignity suffered at their teacher's hands. Says Randolph, "It's good to look back and know we were in at the beginning of the revolution which put English agriculture in the prominent position it holds today".

BIBLIOGRAPHY

48

Many authorities have been consulted in the
compilation of this book. Much has also been
read. In general the books below deal with
specific aspects of early farm machinery. and
are commended to anyone interested in finding
out more about any particular topic.

A Century of Traction Engines, W. J. Hughes,
    David & Charles
Traction Engines in Review, Barry J. Finch,
    Ian Allan
Steam Traction Engines, Wagons and Rollers,
    In Colour, Brian Johnson, Blandford Press
Waterloo Ironworks, L. T. C. Rolt,
    David & Charles
Ploughing By Steam, John Haining and
    Colin Tyler, Model & Allied Publications
The English Plough, J. B. Passmore,
    Oxford University Press London:
    Humphrey Milford
The English Farm Wagon, J. Geraint Jenkins,
    Oakwood Press
Discovering Carts and Wagons, John Vince,
    Shire Publications
Early Agricultural Machinery,
    Michael Partridge, Hugh Evelyn
The Book Of The Farm, H. Stephens, 1891
The Land Is Yours, C. Henry Warren,
    Eyre and Spottiswoode
Royal Agricultural Society of England, Journals